PORTRAIT OF A MARKET

For Evelyn
With love,

~~Steve~~

5/31/87

PORTRAIT OF A MARKET

PHOTOGRAPHS OF SEATTLE'S PIKE PLACE MARKET

JOHN STAMETS

WITH TEXT BY STEVE DUNNINGTON

THE REAL COMET PRESS
SEATTLE
1987

To the working people of the Pike Place Market.

Published by arrangement with the photographer, Portrait of a Market is an
original publication of The Real Comet Press, a division of Such A Deal
Corporation. For information: 3131 Western Avenue, #410, Seattle, Washington
98121. Telephone: 206/283/7827

Design: Ed Marquand Book Design
Typography: Scarlet Letters Ltd., Seattle
Printed in Hong Kong by South China Printing Co.

Library of Congress Cataloging-In-Publication Data

First Edition
87 88 89 90 10 9 8 7 6 5 4 3 2 1

Library of Congress Cataloging-in-Publication Data

Stamets, John, 1949-
    Portrait of a market.

    1. Pike Place Market (Seattle, Wash.)—Pictorial
works. 2. Markets—Washington (State)—Seattle—
Pictorial works. 3. Seattle (Wash.)—Description—
Views. 4. Seattle (Wash.)—Social life and customs—
Pictorial works. I. Dunnington, Steve, 1950-
II. Title.
HF5472.U7S48   1987   381'.18'0979777   87-4746
ISBN 0-941104-17-6 (pbk.)

PREFACE

This book began in the fall of 1985 when Philip Wohlstetter of Invisible Seattle suggested that I take my panoramic camera down to the Pike Place Market to illustrate an article he was writing on "real" markets vs. financial markets. My plan was to take two rolls of film at Pike Place and two rolls over in some big bank building, and that would be that. As it turned out I rediscovered the Pike Place Market through this camera and went back every week for the next 16 months until this book was done. I never did make it over to the bank building, and Philip has still not finished his article. Nevertheless, thank you Philip.

As much of the Market as these pictures cover, there is much more that is unfortunately not included in this book. In part this is because the Market is such a huge place, and 73 photographs, even in panoramic format, can cover only a fraction of the hundreds of merchants, farmers and craftspeople who do business here. Also, I tended to look at the older parts of the Market, or at least those that seemed most in continuity with the old. These parts of the Market have the deepest roots in history, yet seem most threatened by the pressures of tourism, downtown development and changing demographics. For the record, the photographs in this book were taken between October 1985 and January 1987.

The Widelux camera that I used covers a horizontal angle of 127° using a rotating lens and a slit-scan shutter. This field of view far exceeds that of a conventional wide angle lens, but lacks the spherically shaped distortion of a "fish eye." However, the rotating lens introduces a different type of distortion which causes certain straight lines to appear curved. This effect is most pronounced when viewing a flat storefront up close and straight on, as in the picture of J.D. Almeleh on page 16. If the camera is held level, then the horizon line is straight and level, and there is no vertical line distortion of any kind. However, any horizontal line in the upper part of the picture bends upward, and in the lower part, downward. This distortion is much less noticeable if a scene contains horizontal lines that are relatively short or close to the horizon line. In general I tried to choose locations so that the effects of this distortion would be minimized, while allowing the panoramic format to embrace as much as possible.

In addition to Philip Wohlstetter, I thank photographers Christian Staub, Kim Zumwalt, Ford Gilbreath, Gary Magruder and Barbara Fogel who, knowingly or not, made important contributions in the early stages of the project. Special thanks to Steve Dunnington on keyboard for bringing us the voices of the Market, and to Cathy Hillenbrand of The Real Comet Press for recognizing the potential when there was still hardly anything to see. Finally I thank the people of the Pike Place Market for allowing me into their lives a little bit. Here's what I've been seeing. I'm glad I can give something back.

John Stamets
February 1987

First and Pike.

INTRODUCTION

I'm not an impartial observer of the Pike Place Market. I liked this place the first time I saw it. I liked the irregular geometry of small shops opening onto Pike Place and twisting along narrow warrens into the buildings that lined the street. I liked the farmers with hard hands and sun on their faces lined up behind produce piled on galvanized tables. I liked the craftspeople who set up their paintings and pottery and T-shirts next to them. Mostly I was taken with the colorful blur of humanity and the cloud of fishy, spicey, earthy smells that surrounded it.

It was so American—or at least like my nostalgic idea of America. Small-town friendliness, a slower pace of life, dependable routines, families working hard together, personal service, democratic access to all kinds of people, small farmers bringing the fruits of their labor to the city, independent entrepreneurs and ethnically diverse immigrants strum every chord of the American Dream. It's as though Horatio Alger met up with the do-your-own-thing generation and they decided to go into business together.

I didn't come down here that first time on a field trip. I needed a job while I took some journalism classes. The prospect of getting paid to be out in this welter of humanity was more appealing than being tucked away in some office. I spoke to one of the partners at the newsstand in the Market and he put me on part-time. It soon became clear that there was more work to be done than there was money to pay for it, so they took me on as a partner. I don't know if it says more about me or the Market, but I never expected to stay very long and six years later, I'm still here.

The Market has grabbed a lot of people harder than they expected over the years. These seven acres are, by definition, a place for doing business, but there's something more important going on than just making money. Frank Genzale recalls that after he and his brother bought their first produce stand in the Market, the former owner would park his car across the street and just watch the place for two years after he sold it.

"It's the difference between a business and making a living," observes Frank's father Tony. "The Market is a living." Tony came here in 1927 when his family emigrated from Italy to a farm in south King County. Tony's parents, in-laws, children and grandchildren have all sold at the Market.

The best thing about working here instead of just shopping is getting to know the personalities that started to emerge from the crowd. Having a job on the corner gives me an opportunity to talk with people I could never have met otherwise. I feel rich to know people who had hunted walrus in skin boats with their fathers. I feel rich passing the time with a courtly older man from North Carolina who played outfield for the Hollywood Stars in baseball's Pacific Coast League during the 1920s.

For many of our customers at the newsstand, the "Big War" will always be the one in 1917. Some of them share memories of countries that no longer exist on any map. They share a world of horse-drawn transportation and no airplanes. Many have passed on since they began coming by the stand. Children who first came as newborn babies with their parents now go to school.

There is something frustrating about these encounters too. The variety of races and ages and backgrounds makes it easy to assume that there are fantastic stories behind even the most unassuming faces, but there is never enough time to know more than a tiny fraction of them. Verbal exchanges on the street are always short but never "small" talk. One friendly patron reached for his paper and exposed the blue-black numbers tattooed on his arm in a Polish concentration camp. We didn't say much about it but it wasn't small.

When Queen Elizabeth was visiting Seattle, one of her go-fers stopped by the stand for the day's papers. When Geraldine Ferraro was campaigning, she stopped by the corner and signed autographs. On other mornings, we've had to drag people out who were sleeping between the newsstand and the wall. The Market doesn't eliminate prejudice, but the range of humanity in the Market demonstrates constantly that crude categories like race, age, ethnic background and style of dress are not very helpful indicators of human character.

The fact that the Market is on the street accounts for much of this spontaneous democracy. It also means that it shares the problems of any large downtown area. We made a rule at the newsstand early on that people could look at the magazines but they couldn't talk to them. Even so, angry folks with hospital tags on their wrists are a fact of life. They rail at the magazines, the lampposts or anything else that gets in their way.

Down-and-out alcoholics bum change until they get enough for a bottle and then drink until they fall down. They lie in their own puddles until the county detox wagon hauls them away and they recover sufficiently to start the whole cycle again. It's not romantic and it's not picturesque to watch this process repeat itself over and over. These are the cases that make customers shake their heads and think twice about coming to a place where they have to rub up against this type of experience.

There's another population here that often gets lumped in with the craz   and the drunks, but they're very different. One might find this second group of people ''slow'' or ''off'' or just so easygoing that they trade sporadic pay for the luxury of hanging out, but they're an important part of the Market community. They help with deliveries, sweep floors, haul garbage, scrounge empty boxes, clean vegetables. They see that cardboard is recycled and get the old bread and produce to soup kitchens that can put it to use. In exchange, they get a couple of bucks or something to eat or sometimes even a place to sleep in a storeroom after hours. More important than the money is that they know people in this neighborhood and what they do is valued.

A unique network of services and suppliers has grown up around the Market. Charlie makes the rounds in his old blue truck, recycling the empty bottles from Market bars and restaurants. Another guy comes by at night for the cardboard left over from the day's boxes. A knife sharpener parks his step van on Pike Street every Tuesday to take care of the butchers, fish sellers and restaurants in the area.

The thing that makes this community possible are the hundreds of small, independent vendors crammed into just four blocks. They don't have to consult with their board of directors before they hire somebody off the street to help unload a truck. The farmers don't check their liability with the insurance company before they just leave the stuff that won't last another day for whoever needs it. If a vendor wants to buy a small lot of basil from a local grower, he doesn't need a policy memorandum to do it.

You cannot buy anything without talking to somebody. Haggling is not appreciated, but what you pay always depends on how much you buy, the season, the time of day, your attitude, who you buy it from, whether they know you and what kind of mood they're in. If you need tomatoes for sauce, the overly ripe ones that were culled from the display because they had some soft spots would be perfect. The vendor would rather sell them cheaply than throw them in the dumpster, but there are no signs explaining this fact. You have to ask.

Human contact attends every transaction in the Market. Human attention surrounds everything that's for sale. Every day the Market is literally created anew. Each morning the produce displays are set up piece by piece. Fishmongers lay out fresh white beds of ice for shining silver rungs of salmon. Farmers who have planted, cultivated and picked their crops clean them off, trim them, tie them into bunches, and lay them out in neat piles on the galvanized tables. Craftspeople haul their goods out of lockers in time for nine o'clock roll call. At night, the Market is taken apart and cleaned up for the next day.

This daily routine has been going on for 80 years. Generations have grown up performing this ritual. Dinah Yokoyama began her stint in the Market in a banana box behind the fruit stand that her parents owned and worked. When she was old enough to get out of the box, she worked with her folks, and then helped her brothers when they took over Pike Place Fish. Now she's raising children of her own.

Other families now in the Market who have been here for at least two generations include the Amons, Apostols, Bryants, Calvos, Camerotas, Cohens, Cruz's, D'Ambrosios, DeLaurentis, Desimones, Dykes, Genzales, Greenblats, Hanadas, Harts, Kuzaros, Lebows, LoPriores, Manns, Manzos, Molinas, Ordonios, Primeros, Rilleras, Roos's, Signeys, Verdis, Vilorias, the Levys of City Fish, the Levys of Three Girls' Bakery and Viola Brown the lady barber. There are undoubtedly others that I've missed.

As you can tell from the names, the Market has a strong immigrant tradition. Many families from the Avellino region of Italy came to farms in south Seattle. They began selling their produce in the Market before they could speak English. Sephardic Jews from the eastern Mediterranean came to the Market after the First World War to work at the produce stands and fish markets. Jacob David "Jack" Almeleh began selling produce at First and Pike the day he arrived from the Isle of Rhodes. He was 17 when he arrived in Seattle with his brothers. He's 83 now and still selling

several days a week for Frank Genzale at Quality Produce.

Japanese farmers were a strong force in the Market, despite the difficulty they had with laws against Asian immigration and land ownership. Many Filipinos followed them to this area as agricultural workers around the time of the Second World War. As they got land of their own, they became another major ethnic thread in the Market fabric.

More recently, Hmong and Mien farmers from Laos sell produce on the day tables and Korean immigrants are now running four of the ten permanent vegetable stands. There are businesses here with ethnic roots in Afghanistan, Africa, Bolivia, China, France, Germany, Greece, India, Indonesia, Ireland, Israel, Italy, Japan, Malaysia, Mexico, Pakistan, the Philippines, Scandinavia, South America, Turkey, Viet Nam, and Yugoslavia.

This melting pot in the Market hasn't been an undiluted draught of the milk of human kindness. One of our customers at the newsstand recalls growing up in the 1930s. He and his family couldn't go into restaurants along Pike Street because they were black. During World War II, Pete Hanada's family, along with nearly everyone else of Japanese ancestry, was ordered into concentration camps in Eastern Washington and Idaho, even though Pete's father Toichi had been raising produce and selling it in the Market since 1919.

"I gave a guy power of attorney when we left," Pete says bitterly. "When I come back in 1945, I had to pay him $1,000 to get my stuff back." The Hanadas were one of the few Japanese families able to return to their land. In spite of their hardship, they also came back to the Market.

It doesn't redress any of the wrongs that their family suffered, but it's a nice footnote to life in the Market that when the Hanadas returned, they made friends with a young butcher named Don Kuzaro who had fought the Japanese in the Pacific. Thirty years later, Pete's niece Diana, who helped sell their produce on the farmers' tables, got married to Don Jr. who was learning meat-cutting from his dad across the aisle at Don and Joe's Meats.

One of the most complex aspects of Market history is the relationship of this freewheeling, independent community of small business people to the Seattle city bureaucracy. This relationship began when produce prices increased tenfold from 1906 to 1907, and farmers complained that their commissions from the wholesale middlemen had not risen accordingly. In August of 1907, the city council created a market on Pike Place where farmers could sell directly to the public.

Within three months, the line between the Public Market and private investment was blurred forever. The council designated a parking area for farmers' wagons and provided a policeman to keep order, but it neglected to provide any shelter for farmers and shoppers. Businessman Frank Goodwin owned the Leland Hotel on the western edge of Pike Place. He filled the need for shelter by building covered stalls north of his hotel. Over the years, he and his nephew Arthur Goodwin built a labyrinth of passageways and shops into the hill between Pike Place and Western Avenue as far north as Stewart Street. The street still belonged to the city, but the buildings belonged to the Goodwin Real Estate Company and other private developers.

In 1922, the city council decided that the farmers' wagons had to come off the street in order to make way for increased automobile traffic. Goodwin offered to cover the sidewalk in front of his property and build display tables for the displaced farmers, but he wanted the right to rent the middle of this area to retailers on a monthly basis.

Market farmers complained that this turned the best public selling area over to a private individual. Goodwin argued that without his efforts, there wouldn't even be a Public Market to defend. The farmers brought suit, but the city eventually vacated the disputed sidewalk in favor of

Goodwin and got the covered farmers' tables along the west edge of Pike Place in return. The block of permanent "high stalls" which Goodwin was permitted to rent out still stands in the middle of the Market's Main Arcade.

The only portions of the Pike Place Market that remained truly public were the farmers' tables which the city rented out by the day. The rest of the Market was run as a family business by the Goodwins and then by farmer-entrepreneur Joe Desimone, who acquired a controlling share of the company's stock in 1933. The arrangement worked well until the Second World War, when many workers left the Market for the military or better-paying defense jobs and farmers of Japanese ancestry were interned in concentration camps. The total farmer permits dropped from 515 in 1939 to 53 ten years later.

With the drop-off in business, revenues weren't sufficient to cover necessary maintenance. The Market buildings started to show their age. In 1964, the city council voted to replace the Market with a 3,000-car parking structure containing restaurants, a hotel and office tower sites. At that time University of Washington architecture professor Victor Steinbrueck helped form Friends of the Market to resist the Market's destruction, but by May, 1971, the federal government approved funding for the replacement plan. In a last-ditch effort to preserve the Market, the Friends succeeded in getting Seattle voters to declare the seven acres a historical district by a three-to-two margin. The vote cleared the way for the city to acquire about three-fourths of the privately held property in the new district and to channel nearly 60 million dollars of federal money into restoring the Market structures instead of tearing them down.

What used to happen on a handshake with the Goodwins or the Desimones now had to be hammered into public policies, leases and rules. The voter referendum created the Market Historical Commission to decide what new uses and designs were consistent with the district's past. The city council created the Pike Place Market Preservation and Development Authority to manage city property on a day-to-day basis.

By the time citizens voted to preserve the area's history, the city had already shut down the Market brothels and betting parlors. There were no dime-a-dance halls or vaudeville shows anymore. Speakeasies were obsolete as soon as Prohibition was repealed.

In the late 1960s, the port moved all of its cargo-loading from the main waterfront near the Market to mechanized facilities several miles away. The longshore-men's hiring hall moved too, trailing seamen's bars and cheap cafes in its wake.

Many of the inexpensive rooms in the area where single men could wait for a ship or a construction job were closed by tighter fire codes. The Market now provides about 500 low and medium income units within its boundaries, but just beyond, rooms that went for two hundred dollars per month ten years ago have been replaced by two-hundred-thousand-dollar condominiums.

Market farmers have felt the pinch too. They face the same problems as small farmers everywhere, with the added factor that much of their land is close to downtown Seattle. Urban sprawl means higher taxes and increased pressure to sell. New farmers are carving out niches that didn't exist ten years ago by selling organically grown produce, processed jellies, vinegars and flowers crafted into wreaths and centerpieces.

No referendum can turn back the hands of time. Places with an air of danger like the Victrola Tavern, the Hideout and the old Place Pigalle closed in the 1970s. "If you hung out at any of those places long enough, you'd either get beat up or laid or both," recalls former bartender Gary Kennedy. You'd wait considerably longer for either eventuality at the new Place Pigalle that opened on the

same site in 1982. It is a wonderful restaurant with fine food, a great view and attentive service. It's altogether pleasant, but the seedy element of adventure is gone.

Times and tastes have changed. I don't know all the reasons why. Things cost more. People are more materialistic. That old looseness seems harder to come by. Something vital is still pulling people to the Market, though—the family pasts, the entrepreneurial spirit, the openness of the place—or maybe the concentration and variety of people who are here just naturally attract more people. The Market is still a place where small owner–operators can start a business without much capital. The Historical Commission has succeeded in keeping out chains where the owner is not on the premises. This area hasn't turned into a contrived festival mall for "leisure shopping experiences" but the pressure is always there to "improve" the Market according to the retail trend of the day. People love the idea of farmers selling their produce in the Market, but not as many of us are willing to fight traffic and crowds in order to do our regular food shopping here.

I don't know what will happen to the spirit of the Market. I think the best way of carrying what is valuable into the future is to appreciate the value of what we have today. These photos by John Stamets do a wonderful job of helping us do that.

Steve Dunnington
Seattle   1987

I'm indebted to hundreds of Market merchants, farmers, craftspeople, residents and shoppers for sharing their experiences in the Market and helping to create mine. The book *The Pike Place Market—People, Politics and Produce* by Alice Shorett and Murray Morgan was a valuable source for many of the historical facts in this introduction.

Corner of Pike Street and Pike Place.

"Before, mostly we can sell lots of vegetables. This time, no more," says Sabina Molina, who farms in Kent, Washington, with her husband Alex. "My customers, before, they ask for cucumbers but we give them up. Their kids are growing up and nobody is making pickles anymore. That's why we changed to dried flowers.

"The farm is good if you know how to plant. You work, you grow old, you get the money a little bit. Summertime, we are here every day. I braid the garlic at night when I'm watching TV, then I get up 5 o'clock, come here 6 o'clock.

"We sent our kids to college from here, now they have jobs. They don't want to farm. For me, it's more fun to stay in the Market, more people to talk with."

Economy Arcade.

Jacob David ''Jack'' Almeleh began selling produce the day he arrived in the
Market from the Isle of Rhodes, Turkey, nearly 70 years ago. Besides selling
produce, he served as president of his synagogue, taught Hebrew school and
published a newspaper called Progress. In the 1940s, his Hebrew students
included Seby Nahmias from the newsstand. A generation later, he taught Jack
Levy and his sister Zelda Dixon who now own Three Girls Bakery.

    ''A lot of people come around and say, 'Jack, you're educated, why do
you stay around the Market?''' he muses. ''I'm satisfied with what I'm doing. I
like to meet people. I like to joke with them. People, that's my business.''

Frank's Quality Produce on Pike Place.

Corner Produce.

Corner Market Building on Pike Place.

Alan Brenner delivers bread for Brenner Brothers Bakery, started by his grandfather in 1902. ''I used to come down here with my dad when he made his deliveries during summers and Saturdays,'' Alan remembers. ''A lot of these people I've known since I was a kid, but it's getting more corporate. You've got to worry more about your bottom line. I miss the characters, but I still feel comfortable down here.''

"My dad used to come down here by horse and wagon," recalls farmer Pete Hanada. "He got here by noon, sold out by three. It took him all day, until about six or seven to go back.

"The new generation of shoppers doesn't know anything about a wax bean," Pete laments. "New generation doesn't even know how to cook beets. Old-timers knew what kind of beans they liked. The old ones bought that stuff. The Market's nice now but there's nothing but tourists since the renovation. We answer questions all day long and they don't buy nothing from us."

Pete's daughter Judy works as a nurse but helps on the tables when she can.

Economy Arcade.

"First time I came down here was when I started to deliver bread," recalls Pete DeLaurenti. "My boss said, 'I'm going to show you a nice Italian girl.' Mae had a beautiful smile. The next Sunday was a big Italian picnic in Renton. We danced, I took her home, we got married."

Pete and Mae bought her mother's grocery store in 1943 and changed the name to DeLaurenti's. Their son Lou bought the store from them in 1972 and moved it upstairs, but Pete and Mae still work there several days a week.

"What's the difference between all these fish?" is asked by nearly everyone who passes the rows of glittering salmon laid out on their beds of ice in front of Pike Place Fish.

Usually, the sellers on the floor explain the distinctions between chum and king and silver and pink and coho and chinook very patiently, but the routine does get old. At the end of a particularly trying day, one of the fishmongers' answer to that question had boiled down to a single word—"chromosomes."

"This is a family business," says Kari Kuo who helps out at the House of Jade on Saturdays. "It's fun meeting different people from all over the world. Sometimes it's difficult to communicate because of all the different languages. Sometimes you have to use hand signs or write down the price. "After I showed her the earrings, she bought them."

Seby Nahmias carried a .22 caliber pistol back when he was selling papers by himself at First and Pike in the 1960s. It was only fired once.

"I gave it to this friend of mine during the busiest part of the day when Bang! she goes off. How did I know he would pull the trigger?" Seby asks. "Shot a hole through the stand, went and ricocheted up off the ceiling. Just lucky nobody was standing there. Two cops who were right down in the Hideout Tavern underneath the ramp here came running up when they heard it. The guy who shot it was gone with the wind, so they gave me a ticket."

First and Pike.

First and Pike.

"When we first came here around 1973, there were people milling around all
hours of the day and night," says Jack Hunt, owner of Custom Tattoo. "There
were merchant seaman bars, penny arcades, movie houses and at least two
other tattoo shops along First Avenue. That's all changed now. Without the
military and the turnover of bodies, it's slowly going downhill. How many
tattoos can you give somebody?"

Joseph Brown puts a smile on his music around the Market. He was playing his saxophone on the corner the week the national Elks convention descended on Seattle. Their presence sparked a spontaneous street song from Joseph which went, in its entirety, "Has anybody seen a black Elk?"

Joseph liked the song so much, he sang it as he walked the length of the Main Arcade. His Market fans were tickled by the tune and the obvious joy Joseph was getting from the irony in his musical question. Some of the conventioneers, on the other hand, were a little perplexed by the performance.

Isaac ''Ike'' Nahmias, Bill Lundgren and Lois Brown at First and Pike. Lois calls
herself Mae West because she likes the actress's style. She comes down to the
Market every afternoon to pass the time with the sons and daughters she's
''verbally adopted'' on the crafts tables. Even those who haven't heard her
jokes know Mae for her collection of buttons and crocheted beer can hats.

Street musician with dancing puppets.

Mike Patterson has been a craftsperson selling leather goods in the Market since 1971. "First it was a weekend thing. We were just playing. We did all the hippie stuff," he says. "If you haven't gone past the hippie stuff, you can't make it now. Now it's just dealing with what people want. With leather, you've got punkers, country western, yuppies and the hippie flower belts—there's a taste for everything. If you have good material, that's the important thing."

"'Life is for living,' she said before she left,'' is the title of the painting on the
wall of the Market Rummage Hall. Toby Owen originally painted the panel as
part of a construction fence in use while the Market was being renovated.

"Every Saturday during the 1920s, my family used to park by the Armory and walk through the Market," remembers Herman Helmun from behind a pile of hats waiting for his attention in the Eclipse Hat Shop. "There used to be a stage in the Municipal Market on the other side of Western where they'd have vaudeville. We'd always aim to do our shopping in time to get there.

"There was a guy in the North Arcade who used to grind fresh horseradish right there on the spot. We used to stand next to him and see who could go the longest without crying."

The sign remains, but the Loback's Meat Company space has been leased out to
other tenants since 1985. The last family member to work in the Market was
Dennis Loback who began as a meat cutter in 1953. He remembers the night
that the cashier wrapped the payroll in white paper and accidentally threw it
out with the garbage. "Before you knew it there were 17 butchers out there
going through the garbage until we finally found the payroll," Dennis recalls.
"I think the bums pushed it aside because it didn't look like food. That was
quite a sight."

Joe Darby, Don Kuzaro Sr. and Don Jr. at Don and Joe's Meats. "My dad
bought the business with my Uncle Joe," explains Don Jr. "I started working
here as a cleanup kid when I was about 17. I bought it from them in 1986.

"I had a great opportunity to work with my father until he retired. He
was working so hard when I was growing up that I hardly knew him. Working
together brought our family together."

Looking east up Pike Street.

The "downstairs" of the Market consists of four levels that spill down the hillside between Pike Place and Western Avenue towards the Sound. Over the years, the many Lower Level tenants have included a post office, library, doughnut shop, creamery, lard rendering plant, print shop and "Madame Nora's Temple of Destiny."

The Market renovation in the 1970s brought new floors, lighting and shop walls for the antique stores, gift shops and other specialty stores that occupy the space now.

"Ben the Market barber was my ideal," recalls Dick Busch, who runs the Balcony Barber Shop with Mondo Canales. "He just wanted to be good people, raise his family, maybe sell a bottle of Stephen's Hair Tonic once in a while, maybe not."

Dick blames "style shops" for the disappearance of many barbershops in the area. "In a style shop, people are so involved with themselves. And you're trying to get them to worry even more about themselves so that you can sell more products," he says. "It's not my cup of tea. I just try to give a good haircut at a good price."

"If you didn't like people, you'd be an absolute failure here," says Rita Dyke
of Rita's Books. "I treat each customer as though they were the only one.
People are sick and tired of being ignored.

"I think of everyone being honest even though things do get stolen. If I
didn't, I'd have high blood pressure. It's easy to get along provided you're not
afraid, and I'm not."

"The feeling in the Market reminds me of Afghanistan—very crowded and interesting down here," says Anwar Popal, owner of Afghan Crafts.

"I definitely think about going back. Nothing can compare with your home town. You walk really proud. People are so close to each other, you never feel alone.

"Here, I can't find people. You call them up two weeks before a party and they say, 'I'll see if I have time.' Everyone is working or studying. Even if you go for a visit, you have to call."

First Lower Level.

"The secret is part of the sale" promises a sign on the Magic Shop wall. Even for those who don't buy anything, Sheila "Magic Lady" Lyon or her husband Darryl "The Amazing" Beckmann are likely to display their magic secrets in a spontaneous show.

"We had 400 school trips through here last year," explains Sheila. "The kids' tour of the Market involves the candy store, the comic book place and the Magic Shop. I think I've probably squirted every kid in the Northwest with disappearing ink."

"I pretend I'm an entrepreneur. I'm really the smallest kind of businessman you can be," says Richard "Dick the Dollman" Iverson of Grandpa's Attic. "I taught history for 30 years. Now I'm retired, but I like contact with the public.

"I came to the Market 15 years ago when I had a shop on the Mezzanine Level, before renovation. There was an old woman who used to come in and sleep in my shop after hours. By just stepping over the counter, you could do that very easy.

"I'm afraid that if rents keep going up, old-fashioned businesses like myself with lots of things for small amounts of money will be forced out."

"Ladies here like hearing what era they're in when they pick something up," observes Tracy Kay of Market Space 31 on the Market's First Lower Level. "I like to give them a little history on it."

Before he opened Market Miscellaneous in 1985, Konrad Murray sold crafts on the day tables, worked at other businesses in the Market and served on the staff of the Pike Place Market Preservation and Development Authority. He even took a turn as a street musician. ''The only role I haven't played in the Market is farmer,'' he notes, standing behind a case of what he describes as ''the Cadillacs of rhinestone jewelry.''

Victor Steinbrueck Row, Main Arcade.

Tina Ordonio has been selling produce in the Market ever since she married
Rufino Ordonio and he brought her to Seattle from the Philippines in 1949.

"Only three, four years ago they wouldn't let us sell flowers in my
section," Tina says. "I kept nagging them and nagging them. After they get
tired with me, they approved it.

"We used to sell more vegetables, but if you sell your beans for one
dollar, the customers say it's too high. When we sell the flowers, they never
complain. I like to switch to flowers because it's lighter for me to handle."

North Arcade.

At the Market Street Fair and other Northwest crafts fairs, Mee Vang sells the Hmong needlework that his wife, sister and mother learned to make in their native Laos. During the week, he works as a nursing assistant and his wife works for Seattle City Light.

"We like to show everybody our culture," Mee explains.

Post Alley.

Newer Market farmers such as Susan Gronlund and Joel Rankin have the advantage that their products are not as perishable as fresh produce. Joel and his wife Ann sell cider from his parents' orchard in Cashmere, Washington. Susan blends aromatic vinegars with the herbs she grows on her farm in Fall City.

"Day-to-day optimism is what keeps you going," she says. "You never know from one day to the next what the public is going to buy. Farmers have to be much more sophisticated these days in a business sense."

Flower Row merchant.

Market Street Fair.

Music audience at Victor Steinbrueck Park.

Market Street Fair.

Post Alley at Pine Street.

Post Alley at Stewart Street.

Kurt Magnuson helps a customer at City Fish in the North Arcade. City Fish was started in 1918 to combat profiteering on fish sales during the First World War. The State Fisheries Commission gave hatchery salmon to the city, which sold them at cost through the municipally owned fish market. David Levy bought the stand in 1926. His sons Jack and Gary took it over from him and now his grandson, also named David Levy, manages the store.

North Arcade.

Pincus Almeleh working on the Main Arcade.

Central Casting couldn't have come up with a better rendition of a solid, old-country peasant woman than Pasquelina Verdi. She is the Real Thing—right down to the dirt caked under her broad fingernails. For 27 years, her rosy cheeks, hair tied back in a kerchief, playful good humor, gold-rimmed smile and thick Italian accent have had as much to do with making her a Market landmark as the vegetables she brings to the day tables.

"It's my life," says Pasquelina. "I stay home, I miss the people."

She has been staying home more often lately due to back problems, but Pasquelina's son Mike and his wife Sue (at right) continue to work her South Seattle farm and bring their produce down to the Market.

Since she started the Oriental Mart on Pike Place in 1973, Mila Apostol has never had to hire an employee. The store has been as much a place to raise her six children as it has been a source of income. "My youngest child was about three when I started," Mila recalls. "I had a playpen where I would put him to sleep. In the afternoon, he would just stand up on the chair and holler 'Everybody buys.' Now, when business is slow, I ask him to do it again and he just tells me, 'Oh mom.'

"I'm really proud of my kids in the Market. Even if my children don't stay here, it has given them very good training."

Dave Sweeny and owner Rick Mann at Old Friends on the Second Lower Level.
Rick named the store in honor of the old-timers who come in to pass the time.
They're the ones who told him about the ghost who floats through the
Market's lower levels. Some say she is the daughter of Chief Sealth, others say
she is the shade of a woman who fell through a Market floor and died.

    Rick has never seen the ghost himself but he mentioned her to a news-
paper columnist who first published the story. A national tabloid newspaper
embellished the account, and last Halloween, Rick repeated it so many
times for the television cameras that now he's sick of the whole thing.

"We get new stuff all the time," says Charlie Swanberg in his tiny gift shop in the Market's Main Arcade. "When Mt. St. Helens went, I couldn't believe it; then this Michael Jackson stuff went over big. Now you can't give it away.

"In a place like this, you get a lot of young people. Most of our customers can't afford expensive stuff so we price a lot of it at 93 cents—a dollar with the tax."

Sasquatch by sculptor Richard Beyer.

"There are lots of bus fare and beans days," admits Ivy Rice, who has been
selling her candles in the Market for several years. "But on any day there's
always the potential that sales are going to be really good. I love that sense of
the unknown.

"I like being down here with the whole mix of people from ladies with
five-thousand-dollar furs to the most destitute transient. I don't know if the
Market has improved my opinion of human nature but it's made the picture a
lot clearer."

"The gift of art. It's inside my blood. I can't take it out," says Demetrios
"Mr. D" Moraitis, displaying his Venus de Milo molded from *gyros,* the ground
lamb used in Greek sandwiches. "Something comes and that's it. I make
experiments, studies with anything I have in my hand—meat, snow, anything.
My curiosity is so strong.

   "I made Socrates and his family in the snow last Thanksgiving. Socrates
got his knowledge from the public market at Athens. That was his learning and
teaching spot. Same thing with this market. I don't have to move from my
stand to search for things. I don't have to have a doctor's degree in sociology.
The Market is the best place to learn about people."

At the Athenian Cafe in the Main Arcade.

Pike Place Fish Company.

Crab steamer in the Sanitary Market Building.

The south entrance to the Market at First and Pike is favored by groups that want to get in touch with "the masses." In this case, it's the Revolutionary Communist Party (left) selling their newspaper, but you're as likely to find evangelists seeking converts, charitable groups seeking donations, candidates looking for votes, politicians looking for exposure or corporations that want public reaction to their cigarettes, aspirin and candy bars.

Mary Preus raises vegetables, herbs and flowers on her farm across Puget
Sound. At Christmas time, she dries her flowers and weaves them into
wreaths. She also raises two girls as a single parent.

"I like to bring my kids down," she says. "My daughter who is almost
nine sometimes works for the other sellers. She's learning how to get along in
situations with all kinds of people. The Laotian farmers who set up next to us
told the girls about escaping from their country. That's real in a way that
reading about it could never be."

Floor tiles with contributors' names engraved on them were sold in order to
repave the Market's arcades.

Workers on a break, Economy Arcade.

Tattooist.

Mas Kajioka and helper shortly before he sold the Wonder Freeze in 1986.

John Stamet's photographs have captured much of the Northwest. His freelance work has appeared in the *New York Times*, the *Los Angeles Times*, *Sierra Club West Magazine*, *Sunset Magazine* and other publications. This is John's first book.

Steve Dunnington is a journalist and co-owner of the Pike Place Market newsstand, Read All About It. His articles have appeared in many Northwest publications. This is his first book.